Contents

Songs

What fun is in store for you today! This RECORDER FUN!™ SONGBOOK will have you playing the recorder quickly and easily while you learn to play your favorite Christmas songs.

ISBN 0-634-08223-X

7777 W. BLUEMOUND RD. P.O. BOX 13819 MILWAUKEE, WI 53213

E-Z Play Today® Music Notation © 1975 by HAL LEONARD CORPORATION
E-Z PLAY and EASY ELECTRONIC KEYBOARD MUSIC are registered trademarks of HAL LEONARD CORPORATION.

Visit Hal Leonard Online at
www.halleonard.com

GETTING STARTED

HOLDING THE RECORDER

Here is how to hold the recorder. The mouthpiece rests on your lower lip, just like a drinking straw, with only a little c it actually going inside your mouth. Be sure that all of the finger holes line up on the front of the recorder as shown i the picture.

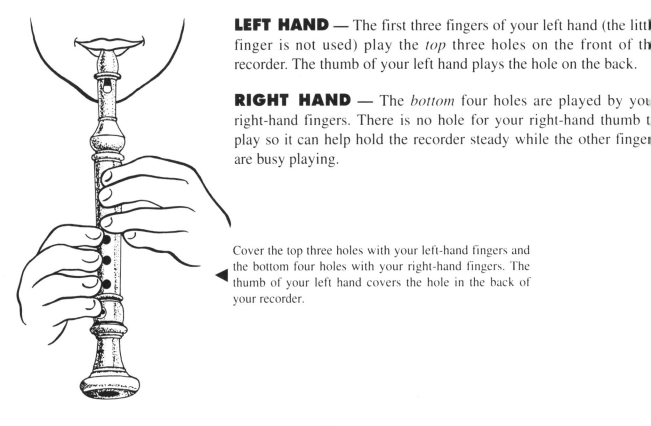

LEFT HAND — The first three fingers of your left hand (the littl finger is not used) play the *top* three holes on the front of th recorder. The thumb of your left hand plays the hole on the back.

RIGHT HAND — The *bottom* four holes are played by you right-hand fingers. There is no hole for your right-hand thumb t play so it can help hold the recorder steady while the other finger are busy playing.

Cover the top three holes with your left-hand fingers and the bottom four holes with your right-hand fingers. The thumb of your left hand covers the hole in the back of your recorder.

MAKING A SOUND

To make a sound on the recorder blow gently into the small opening at the top of the mouthpiece. You can change thi sound by covering different holes with your thumb and fingers. For example, when you cover all of the thumb an finger holes you will get a low, quiet sound. When only one or two holes are covered the sound will be higher an much louder.

Here are some tips for getting the best possible sound out of your recorder:

Always blow gently into the mouthpiece — Breathe in and then gently blow into the mouthpiece as if you were sighing or using a straw to blow out a candle. Remember, always blow gently.

Leaks cause squeaks — Play the holes using the pads of your fingers and thumb (not the tips). Press against each hole firmly so that it is completely covered and no air can sneak out. Even a tiny leak of air will change a beautiful tone into a sudden squeak!

Use your tongue to start each tone — Place your tongue against the roof of your mouth just behind your front teeth and start each tone that you play by tonguing the syllable "du" or "too" as you blow gently into the recorder.

PLAYING A TONE

Musical sounds are called *tones*. Every tone has a letter name. *Finger charts* are used to show you exactly which holes should be covered in order to play a particular tone. Each circle on these charts represents one of the holes on your recorder. The thumb hole is represented by the circle to the left of the recorder in the chart.

●   means that you should cover that hole.

○   means that that hole should not be covered but left open.

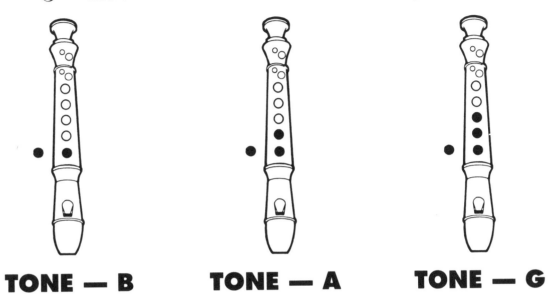

TONE — B   **TONE — A**   **TONE — G**

Use these three tones to play "Mary Had A Little Lamb:"

MARY HAD A LITTLE LAMB

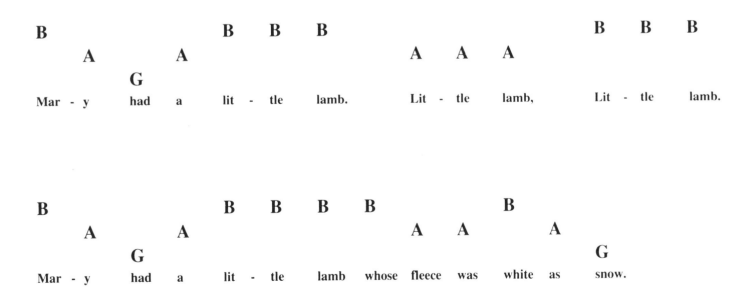

READING MUSIC

Musical notes are an easy way to see everything that you need to know in order to play a song on your recorder:

How high or low — Notes are written on five lines that are called a *staff*. The higher a note is written on the staff the higher it will sound.

How long or short — The color of a note (black or white) tells you if it should be played short or long. The black notes in "Mary Had A Little Lamb" are all one beat long (*quarter notes*). The first three white notes in this song are two beats long (*half notes*) and the last note is four beats long (*whole note*).

How the beats are grouped — The two numbers at the beginning of the song (4/4) are called a *time signature*. This time signature tells you that the *beats* in this song are grouped in fours: **1** 2 3 4 **1** 2 3 4 etc. To help you see this grouping, *bar lines* are drawn across the staff to mark each *measure* of four beats. A *double bar* is used to mark the end of the song.

Now here is how "Mary Had A Little Lamb" looks when it is written in musical notes:

MARY HAD A LITTLE LAMB

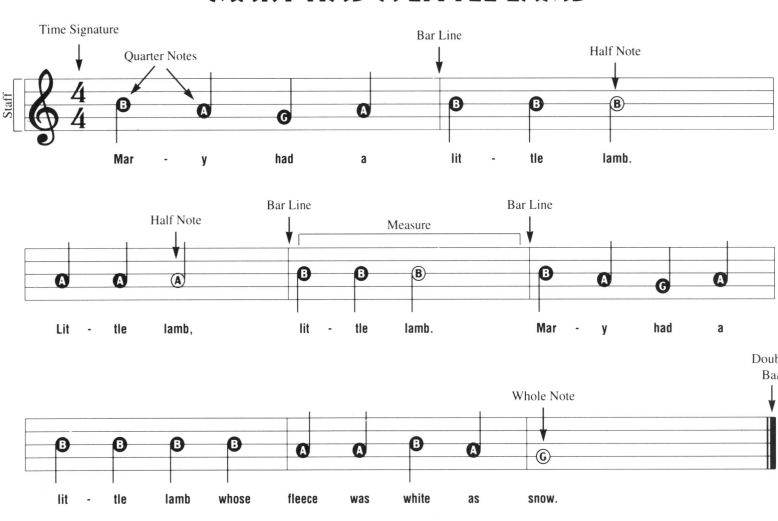

TWO NEW TONES

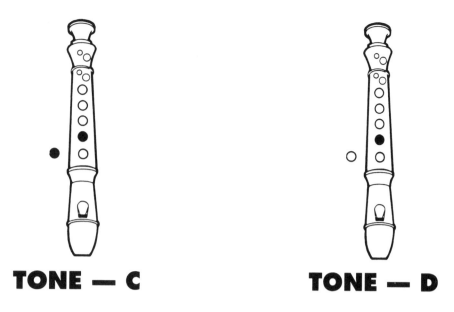

TONE — C   **TONE — D**

AURA LEE

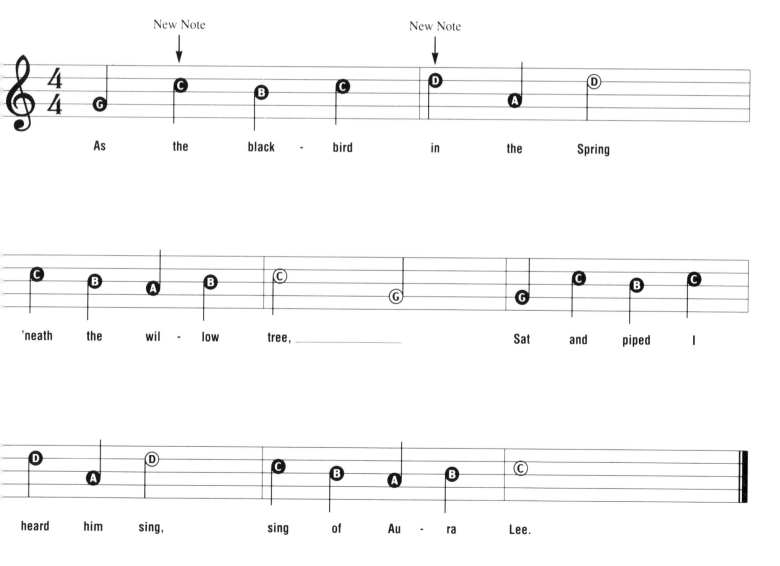

USING YOUR RIGHT HAND

"Twinkle, Twinkle Little Star" uses the tone E. As you can see from the fingering chart, you will use three fingers of your left hand and two fingers of your right to play this tone. The thumb hole is only half filled in (◑). This means that you should "pinch" the hole with your thumb so that only a small part of the hole is left open. Pinching is done by bending your thumb so that the thumbnail points directly into the recorder leaving the top of the thumb hole open.

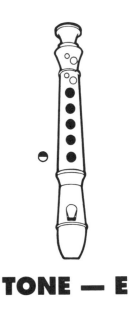

TONE — E

TWINKLE, TWINKLE LITTLE STAR

NOTES AND RESTS

In addition to notes that are one, two or four beats long, other values are possible. Also, *rests* are used to indicate when you should *not* play a tone but be silent. The chart on page 7 will help you identify the different notes and rests that are used in this book.

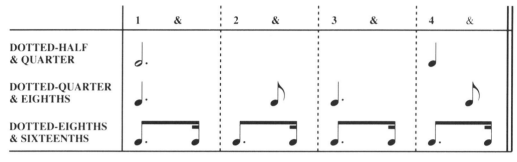

COUNT:

	1	&	2	&	3	&	4	&	NUMBER OF BEATS	REST
WHOLE NOTES									4	
HALF NOTES									2	
QUARTER NOTES									1	
EIGHTH NOTES			(or)						1/2	
& SIXTEENTHS			(or)						1/4	

DOTTED NOTES ARE 1 1/2 TIMES THE NORMAL LENGTH:

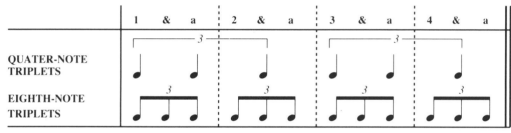

	1	&	2	&	3	&	4	&
DOTTED-HALF & QUARTER								
DOTTED-QUARTER & EIGHTHS								
DOTTED-EIGHTHS & SIXTEENTHS								

TRIPLETS ARE SPREAD EVENLY ACROSS THE BEATS:

	1	&	a	2	&	a	3	&	a	4	&	a
QUATER-NOTE TRIPLETS												
EIGHTH-NOTE TRIPLETS												

THIS OLD MAN

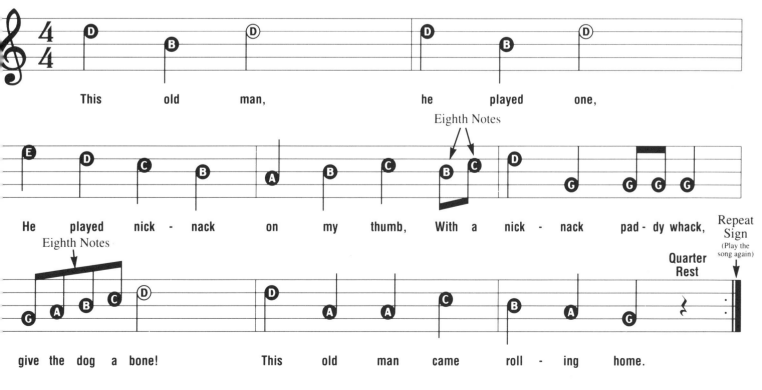

This old man, he played one,

He played nick - nack on my thumb, With a nick - nack pad - dy whack,

Eighth Notes

Eighth Notes

Quarter Rest

Repeat Sign (Play the song again)

give the dog a bone! This old man came roll - ing home.

FINGERING CHART

Some tones have two names (C♯/D♭, D♯/E♭). These are called enharmonics. Even though enharmonic notes look different, they will sound the same.

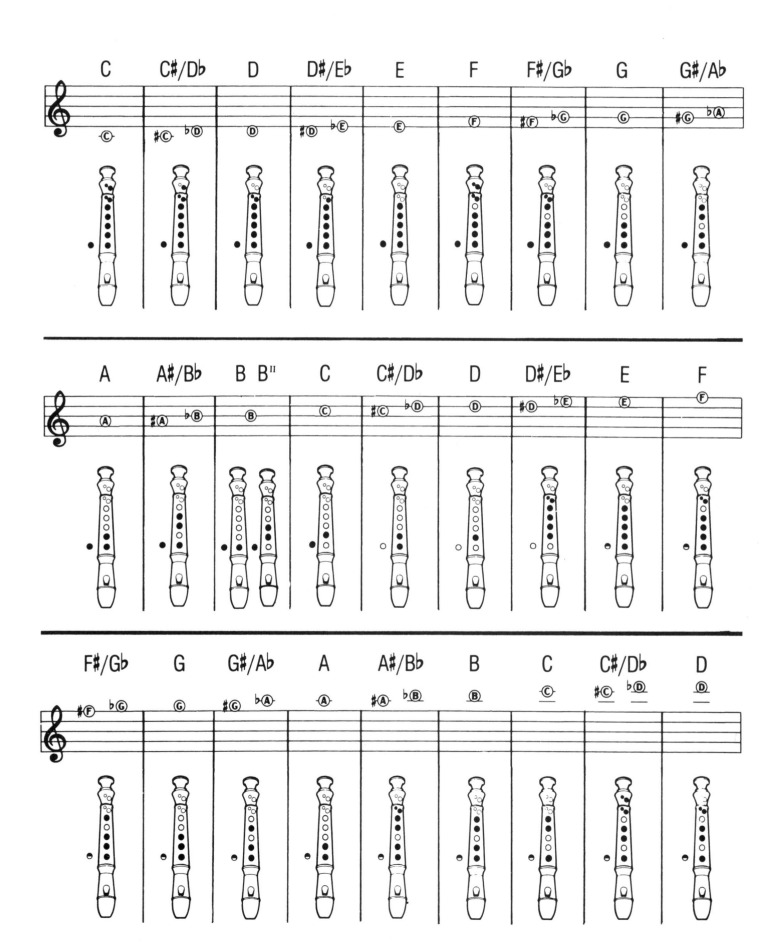

DO YOU HEAR WHAT I HEAR

Words and Music by Noel Regney
and Gloria Shayne

Said the night wind to the lit - tle lamb:
lit - tle lamb to the shep - herd boy:
shep - herd boy to the might - y king:
king to the peo - ple ev - 'ry - where:

Do you see what I see? _____
Do you hear what I hear? _____
Do you know what I know? _____
Lis - ten to what I say! _____

Way up in the sky, lit - tle lamb,
Ring - ing through the sky, shep - herd boy,
In your pal - ace warm, might - y king,
Pray for peace, __ peo - ple ev - 'ry - where.

do you see what I see? _____
do you hear what I hear? _____
do you know what I know? _____
Lis - ten to what I say! _____

A star, a star, danc - ing in the night, with a
A song, a song, high a - bove the tree, with a
A Child, a Child shiv - ers in the cold; let us
The Child, the Child, sleep - ing in the night; He will

tail as big as a kite, with a
voice as big as the sea, with a
bring Him sil - ver and gold. Let us
bring us good - ness and light. He will

tail as big as a kite.
voice as big as the sea.
bring Him sil - ver and gold.

Said the bring us good - ness and light. _____
Said the
Said the

FROSTY THE SNOW MAN

Words and Music by Steve Nelson
and Jack Rollins

HERE COMES SANTA CLAUS
(RIGHT DOWN SANTA CLAUS LANE)

Words and Music by Gene Autry
and Oakley Haldeman

I SAW MOMMY KISSING SANTA CLAUS

Words and Music by
Tommie Connor

LET IT SNOW! LET IT SNOW! LET IT SNOW!

Words by Sammy Cahn
Music by Jule Styne

MERRY CHRISTMAS, DARLING

Words and Music by Richard Carpenter
and Frank Pooler

SANTA CLAUS IS COMIN' TO TOWN

Words by Haven Gillespie
Music by J. Fred Coots

SILVER BELLS
FROM THE PARAMOUNT PICTURE THE LEMON DROP KID

Words and Music by Jay Livingston
and Ray Evans

hear: _____
hear: _____ }

Sil - ver bells, _____

sil - ver bells, _____

it's Christ - mas

time   in   the   cit - y. _____

Ring - a - ling, _____

hear them ring, _____

soon   it   will   be   Christ - mas   day. _____

Strings   of   day. _____

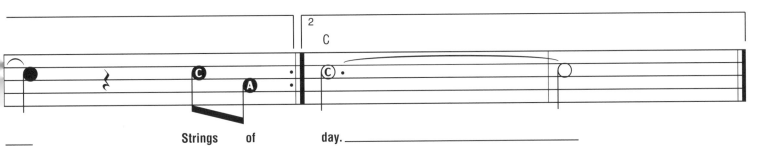

RECORDER FUN!

The recorder is a terrific instrument for children to use to learn music. It's lightweight, portable, sounds great, and can be learned quickly and easily. This fun-filled pack features not only a high-quality, long-lasting recorder, but also a songbook that includes simple and easy-to-follow instructions for a young child or beginner *plus* great coloring pages. Once kids master the basics, they can begin playing their favorite songs from television, films, or characters that they know and love. In no time at all, they'll have learned music basics while having lots of fun!

Recorder Fun! Featuring:

Disney's Aladdin
7 songs, including: One Jump Ahead • Prince Ali • Friend Like Me • A Whole New World • and more! Complete with illustrations.
Pack #00710370   Songbook Only #00710383

Disney's Beauty and the Beast
6 songs, including: Beauty and the Beast • Be Our Guest • Belle • and more! Also features artwork.
Pack #00710359   Songbook Only #00710380

Christmas Songs
15 songs, including: Jingle Bells • Jolly Old St. Nicholas • Silent Night • Up on the Housetop • and more!
Note: this book does not include coloring pages.
Pack #00710372   Songbook Only #00710384

The Disney Collection
6 songs, including: Under the Sea • A Whole New World • Reflection • Can You Feel the Love Tonight • and more!
Pack #00710016

Disney Favorites
7 songs, including: It's a Small World • Under the Sea • Supercalifragilisticexpialidocious • and more!
Pack #00710398   Songbook Only #00710402

Disney's Hercules
6 songs, including: Go the Distance • One Last Hope • Zero to Hero • and more!
Songbook Only #00710013

Disney's The Hunchback of Notre Dame
6 songs, including: The Bells of Notre Dame • Topsy Turvy • and more!
Pack #00710004   Songbook Only #00710007

Disney's The Jungle Book
6 songs, including: The Bare Necessities • I Wanna Be Like You • Trust in Me • That's What Friends Are For • and more!
Pack #00710389   Songbook Only #00710390

Disney's Lady and the Tramp
6 songs, including: Bella Notte • The Siamese Cat Song • He's a Tramp • Lady • and more!
Pack #00710019   Songbook Only #00710018

Disney's The Lion King
All 5 songs from Disney's animated feature, including: Can You Feel the Love Tonight • Circle of Life • and more!
Pack #00710408   Songbook Only #00710412

Disney's The Little Mermaid
All 7 songs from the soundtrack, including: Under the Sea • Kiss the Girl • Part of Your World • and more!
Pack #00710387   Songbook Only #00710388

Disney's Pinocchio
6 songs, including: When You Wish Upon a Star • Give a Little Whistle • and more!
Pack #00710363   Songbook Only #00710382

Disney's Pocahontas
7 songs, including: Colors of the Wind • Just Around the Riverbend • and more!
Pack #00710002   Songbook Only #00710421

Disney's Snow White and the Seven Dwarfs
6 songs, including: Heigh-Ho • Some Day My Prince Will Come • Whistle While You Work • and more!
Also features artwork.
Pack #00710358   Songbook Only #00710379

Songs for Kids
14 songs, including: London Bridge • This Old Man • Take Me Out to the Ball Game • and more!
Pack #00710393   Songbook Only #00710395

The Sound of Music
7 songs, including: Climb Ev'ry Mountain • Do-Re-Mi • My Favorite Things • and more!
Pack #00710355   Songbook Only #00710381

Disney's Tarzan™
7 songs, including: Trashin' the Camp • Two Worlds • You'll Be in My Heart • and more!
Pack #00710023   Songbook Only #00710024

Disney's The Tigger Movie
7 songs, including: How to Be a Tigger • Round My Family Tree • The Wonderful Thing About Tiggers • and more!
Pack #00710027

The Toy Story Collection
5 songs, including: Woody's Roundup • You've Got a Friend in Me • and more!
Pack #00710028

Disney's Winnie the Pooh
6 songs, including: Winnie the Pooh • Little Black Rain Cloud • Rumbly in My Tumbly • The Wonderful Thing About Tiggers • and more!
Pack #00710017

Big Idea's VeggieTales®
6 songs, including: God Is Bigger • The Hairbrush Song • His Cheeseburger • and more!
Pack #00710030

HAL•LEONARD® CORPORATION
7777 W. BLUEMOUND RD. P.O. BOX 13819 MILWAUKEE, WI 53213
Visit Hal Leonard Online at **www.halleonard.com**